Let's Learn All We Can!

written and illustrated
by P.K. Hallinan

 Ideals Children's Books • Nashville, Tennessee
an imprint of Hambleton-Hill Publishing, Inc.

For Renee Masters,
who has taught so many
You Are Smarter Than You Think
—P.K.

Published by Ideals Children's Books
An imprint of Hambleton-Hill Publishing, Inc.
Nashville, Tennessee 37218

ISBN 1-57102-156-6

"Learning is fun!"
said P.K. to Ben.
"It's all just a matter of
try, try again!"

"I like learning too,"
Jay quickly agreed.
"I'm happy to know
how to spell and to read."

And Jeannie chimed in,
"I completely agree!
If we learn all we can,
we'll be smart as can be!"

So the kids got together
and made a new rule:
they'd try to apply
their best efforts at school.

"It's a great thing to do!"
said Henry to Sue.

In class the next morning
they sat without talking,
then followed instructions—
no groaning or balking.

They asked a few questions
by raising their hands,
and asked them again
if they didn't understand.

And none was too shy
to say, "How, when, or why?"

They added their numbers.
They practiced their letters.
They wrote a short sentence—
the neater, the better.

They worked nice and slowly,
at just the right pace,
then giggled a bit
at all they'd erased.

"Learning," laughed Ben,
"*is* try, try again!"

They probed into science.

They peered into art.

They delved into music
and singing in parts.

They pondered the planets
that circled the sun,
then drew constellations
of stars, just for fun.

They worked on computers
and downloaded files.

They searched like researchers
for bugs in the wild.

They even discovered
how long, long ago
dinosaurs traveled
the plains to and fro!

And high in the sky
pterodactyls flew by!

They practiced their soccer
as never before,
because physical fitness
means more than the score.

And as Jay explained,
"Hey, it's only a game!"

At home they did homework,
with gusto and glee.
At school the next day,
they were sharp as could be.

"Learning is great!"
said Jeannie to Jay,
"I'm going to learn
a bit more every day!"

And Henry concurred,
"That's a really good plan!
Let's give school our best...

"Let's learn all we can!"